THE
CHRISTMAS PAGEANT

PLAYERS
CHILDREN JUST LIKE YOU

SETS & COSTUMES BY

TOMIE dePAOLA

THE
CHRISTMAS PAGEANT

illustrated by Tomie de Paola

text from the stories of
Matthew and Luke

FONTANA
PICTURE LIONS

The Christmas story re-told through the acting of a children's
pageant. Full-colour illustrations by award-winning artist Tomie de Paola.

First published in Great Britain 1979 by Methuen Children's Books Ltd
First published in Picture Lions 1981
by William Collins Sons & Co Ltd
14 St James's Place, London SW1

Illustrations and cover copyright © 1978 by Tomie de Paola
Text copyright © 1978 by Winston Press Inc

Printed in Great Britain
by William Collins Sons & Co Ltd, Glasgow

Long ago, on the very first Christmas night, something wonderful happened. A special baby was born. Many, many people had waited a long time for this baby. Tonight in our play we will celebrate the story of his birth.

Here is how the story began. A woman named Mary and her husband Joseph lived in the town of Nazareth in a place called Galilee. Mary was going to have a baby. She and Joseph knew that this baby would be special. Happily they made many plans for the baby's birth.

Then news came that changed their plans. Their king wanted to know how many people lived in his kingdom. So he asked all the people to go to their home-towns to be counted. Mary and Joseph had to travel from Nazareth to Bethlehem.

The trip was long and hard. It was especially hard for Mary, since it was almost time for her baby to be born. But at last Mary and Joseph arrived in Bethlehem. How crowded it was! Many others had come to be counted, too.

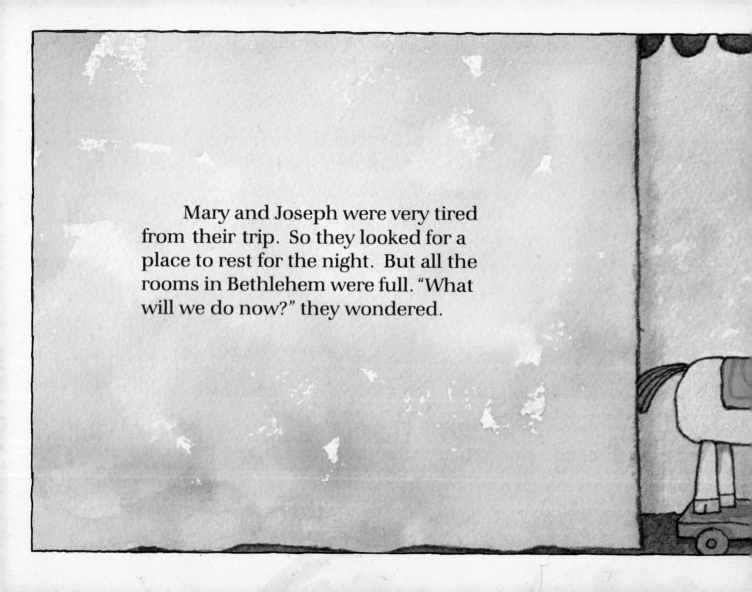

Mary and Joseph were very tired from their trip. So they looked for a place to rest for the night. But all the rooms in Bethlehem were full. "What will we do now?" they wondered.

In Bethlehem the shepherds looked up one street and down the other. At last they found Mary and Joseph and the baby. Jesus was sleeping peacefully on his bed of straw just as the angel had said. When the shepherds saw Jesus they were filled with joy.

Far away, three wise men were looking for the baby, too. They had seen a bright, new star in the East. When they saw the star, they knew that someone special had been born. So the wise men left their faraway lands to search for the baby. They travelled day and night. Each night they looked into the sky to see if the star was still there. Some nights they could not see it. Then they asked, "Where can we find the special child who has just been born?" But no one could tell them.

Then one night the star shone brighter than ever before. "Hurrah!" shouted the wise men. "We must be very near." They followed the star to the place where Mary and Joseph and Jesus were.

As they looked at Jesus, a feeling came over the wise men that made them kneel down before him. Then each wise man offered Jesus a birthday gift.

"I bring you gold," said one.

"I bring you frankincense," said another.

"I bring you myrrh," said the third.

Jesus smiled at them. The wise men could hardly wait to tell everyone about this special child.

These things happened a long time ago. But every year we celebrate the birthday of Jesus, who has shown us how much God loves us and how we should love one another. We are glad you celebrated with us.